United States Government Accountability Office

Report to Congressional Requesters

September 2013

SECURITY CLEARANCES

Additional Mechanisms May Aid Federal Tax-Debt Detection

September 2013

GAO Highlights

Highlights of GAO-13-733, a report to congressional requesters

SECURITY CLEARANCES

Additional Mechanisms May Aid Federal Tax-Debt Detection

Why GAO Did This Study

As of October 2012, about 4.9 million civilian and military employees and contractors held a security clearance. Federal laws do not prohibit an individual with unpaid federal taxes from holding a security clearance, but tax debt poses a potential vulnerability. GAO was requested to review tax-debt detection during the clearance process. GAO examined (1) the number of individuals with unpaid federal taxes, if any, in the OPM security-clearance database and the magnitude of any federal tax debt, and (2) the extent to which federal agencies have mechanisms to detect unpaid tax debt during the security-clearance-approval process.

GAO compared OPM's security-clearance information to the IRS's known tax debts. To provide examples, GAO conducted a detailed review of IRS and security adjudication files of 13 individuals selected, in part, on the basis of tax debt amount and type of security clearance. GAO also reviewed relevant laws and regulations and interviewed officials from the Office of the Director of National Intelligence (ODNI), Treasury, OPM, and three selected federal agencies that represented more than half of the clearance holders in OPM's database.

What GAO Recommends

GAO recommends that ODNI study the feasibility of federal agencies routinely obtaining federal debt information from Treasury for the purposes of investigating and adjudicating clearance applicants, as well as for monitoring current clearance holders' tax-debt status. ODNI agreed with GAO's recommendation.

View GAO-13-733. For more information, contact Stephen M. Lord at (202) 512-6722 or lords@gao.gov.

What GAO Found

About 8,400 individuals adjudicated as eligible for a security clearance from April 2006 to December 2011 owed approximately $85 million in unpaid federal taxes, as of June 2012. This represents about 3.4 percent of the civilian executive-branch employees and contractors who were favorably adjudicated during that period. GAO found that about 4,700 of the approximately 8,400 individuals were federal employees while the remainder was largely federal contractors. Additionally, about 4,200 of these individuals had a repayment plan with the Internal Revenue Service (IRS) to pay back their debt. For this review, GAO used clearance data from the Office of Personnel Management (OPM) Central Verification System (CVS) database. The CVS database does not maintain information on the denial of security clearances on the basis of an individual's nonpayment of federal taxes. Thus, GAO was not able to determine the number of individuals who were denied security clearances for this reason.

Federal agencies have established mechanisms aimed at identifying unpaid federal tax debt of security-clearance applicants; however, these mechanisms have limitations. To detect federal tax debt for clearance applicants, federal investigators primarily rely on two methods: (1) applicants self-reporting tax debts; and (2) validation techniques, such as the use of credit reports or in-person interviews. Each of these methods has shortcomings in detecting unpaid federal tax debts of clearance applicants. For example, credit reports are the primary method for identifying tax debt that was not self-reported, but these reports only contain information on tax debts for which the IRS filed a lien on the debtor's property. According to GAO's analysis, 5 percent of the 8,400 delinquent taxpayers who were favorably adjudicated as eligible for security clearances had a tax lien filed on them. Additionally, federal agencies generally do not routinely review federal tax compliance of clearance holders. There is no process to detect unpaid federal tax debts accrued after an individual has been favorably adjudicated unless it is self-reported, reported by a security manager due to garnishment of wages, or discovered during a clearance renewal or upgrade. GAO's analysis found that 6,300 individuals (approximately 75 percent) accrued their tax debt after approval of the security clearance.

Additional mechanisms that provide large-scale, routine detection of federal tax debt could improve federal agencies' ability to detect tax debts owed by security-clearance applicants and current clearance holders, but statutory privacy protections limit access to this information. Federal agencies may obtain information on federal tax debts directly from the IRS if the applicant provides consent. In addition, federal agencies do not have a mechanism, such as one that the Department of the Treasury (Treasury) uses, to collect delinquent federal debts. Such information could help federal agencies perform routine, automated checks of security-clearance applicants to determine whether they have unpaid federal debts, without compromising statutory privacy protections. Such a mechanism could also be used to help monitor current clearance holders' tax-debt status. Gaining routine access to this federal debt information, if feasible, would better position federal agencies to identify relevant financial and personal-conduct information to make objective assessments of eligibility for security-clearance applicants and continued eligibility of current clearance holders.

_____ United States Government Accountability Office

Contents

Letter		1
	Background	7
	More Than 8,000 Individuals Eligible for Security Clearances Owe about $85 Million in Federal Taxes; About Half Are on Payment Plans with the IRS	15
	Federal Agencies Have Mechanisms to Detect Tax Debt, but Opportunities Exist to Strengthen Detection Capabilities	17
	Conclusions	27
	Recommendation for Executive Action	28
	Agency Comments and Our Evaluation	28
Appendix I	Federal Investigative Standards	30
Appendix II	Revised Adjudicative Guidelines for Determining Eligibility for Access to Classified Information	32
Appendix III	Scope and Methodology	34
Appendix IV	Comments from the Department of Homeland Security	38
Appendix V	Comments from the Office of the Director of National Intelligence	39
Appendix VI	Comments from the Office of Personnel Management	40
Related GAO Products		41

Table

Table 1: Information Gathered in Conducting a Typical
      Investigation to Determine Suitability and Eligibility for a
      Security Clearance   30

Figures

Figure 1: Overview of the Federal Security-Clearance Process   11
Figure 2: Excerpt of Office of Personnel Management (OPM) Form
      SF-86   18

Abbreviations

BMF	Business Master File
COSO	Committee of Sponsoring Organizations of the Treadway Commission
CVS	Central Verification System
DHS	Department of Homeland Security
DOD	Department of Defense
DOE	Department of Energy
e-QIP	Electronic Questionnaires for Investigations Processing
FERDI	Federal Employee/Retiree Delinquency Initiative
FHA	Federal Housing Administration
Fiscal Service	Bureau of the Fiscal Service
FPLP	Federal Payment Levy Program
IMF	Individual Master File
IRS	Internal Revenue Service
IRTPA	Intelligence Reform and Terrorism Prevention Act of 2004
JPAS	Joint Personnel Adjudication System
NMF	Non-Master File
ODNI	Office of the Director of National Intelligence
OPM	Office of Personnel Management
Performance Accountability Council	Suitability and Security Clearance Performance Accountability Council
SAM	System for Award Management
SSN	Social Security number
State	Department of State
TIN	Taxpayer Identification Number
TOP	Treasury Offset Program
Treasury	Department of the Treasury
VA	Department of Veterans Affairs

September 10, 2013

The Honorable Orrin Hatch
Ranking Member
Committee on Finance
United States Senate

The Honorable Tom Coburn
Ranking Member
Committee on Homeland Security and Governmental Affairs
United States Senate

The Honorable Susan M. Collins
United States Senate

The Honorable Dave Camp
Chairman
Committee on Ways and Means
House of Representatives

The Office of the Director of National Intelligence (ODNI) reported that, as of October 2012, over 4.9 million federal employees (civilian and military) and contractors held—or were individuals eligible to hold—a security clearance due to a favorable adjudication.[1] The number of personnel holding clearances underscores the need for security-clearance adjudicators to conduct thorough vulnerability assessments of security-clearance applicants as these clearances may allow government personnel to gain access to classified information that, through unauthorized disclosure, can in some cases cause exceptionally grave damage to U.S. national security. Promulgated under the authority of Executive Order 12968, adjudicative guidelines establish the criteria by which an individual is evaluated for a security clearance determination. The guidelines state that assessments should consider available, reliable information about the person, past and present, favorable and unfavorable, and carefully weigh a number of variables, including whether the applicant has shown an inability or unwillingness to satisfy

---

[1]Office of the Director of National Intelligence, *2012 Report on Security Clearance Determinations* (January 2013).

debts or financial obligations or has failed to file annual required tax returns.[2] Federal law does not expressly prohibit an individual with unpaid federal taxes from being granted a security clearance; however, tax debt does pose a potential vulnerability that must be considered in making a broader determination of whether an applicant should be granted a security clearance. Specifically, federal adjudicative guidelines for determining eligibility for access to classified information state that an individual who is financially overextended is at risk of having to engage in illegal acts to generate funds, and provide that adjudicating officials weigh an individual's debts, such as federal tax debts, as they relate to an individual's financial and personal conduct when making the security-clearance determination.

ODNI is the Security Executive Agent for the federal government. In this role, ODNI is now responsible for developing uniform and consistent policies related to the security-clearance process. The security-clearance process begins with a determination by executive agencies regarding which of their civilian and contractor positions require access to classified information. The individuals identified in those positions must then apply for a security clearance and undergo an investigation. The Office of Personnel Management (OPM) conducts background investigations of security-clearance applicants for most executive agencies. Following the investigation, federal agencies are to determine whether an applicant is eligible for a personnel security-clearance on the basis, in part, of the results of the background investigation. OPM maintains a database of federal employees and contractors adjudicated as eligible for clearances. Individuals approved to hold secret security clearances must undergo a reinvestigation every 10 years, and those approved for top-secret clearances must undergo a reinvestigation every 5 years.[3] We have issued several reports and testimonies on the U.S. government security-

---

[2]Exec. Order No. 12968, 60 Fed. Reg. 40245 (Aug. 7, 2005) and *Revised Adjudicative Guidelines for Determining Eligibility for Access to Classified Information* (Dec. 29, 2005).

[3]OPM officials noted that under the new standards issued in December 2012, it is a 5-year cycle for both types of investigations, with reinvestigations conducted of a random sample of clearance holders. However, these standards have not yet been implemented.

clearance process over the last several years, and highlighted progress being made to improve the timeliness of the clearance process.[4]

You asked us to review the security-clearance process and mechanisms used to identify unpaid federal tax-debt information of applicants, employees, and contractors. For this review, we focused on civilian employees and contractors in the executive branch. We excluded Department of Defense (DOD) employees and contractors and known employees of intelligence agencies from this review.[5] This report answers the following questions: (1) How many individuals with unpaid federal taxes, if any, are in the OPM security-clearance database and what is the magnitude of any unpaid federal tax debt; and (2) To what extent do federal agencies have mechanisms to detect unpaid tax debt during the security-clearance approval process? As part of this work, we are also providing case-study examples of individuals with security clearances with unpaid tax debt to highlight whether the tax debt was revealed during the investigative or adjudicative processes, and, if so, how it was handled during the adjudication. In addition, as agreed with your staff, we are conducting a separate review of DOD security-clearance holders who owe federal taxes and will issue a report on our results next year.

To determine the number of individuals with unpaid taxes in the OPM security-clearance database, as well as determine the magnitude of unpaid federal tax debt, we obtained and analyzed OPM data on individuals eligible for a secret or top-secret security clearance due to a favorable adjudication, either during an initial investigation or a

---

[4]For example, see GAO, *Security Clearances: Agencies Need Clearly Defined Policy for Determining Civilian Position Requirements*, GAO-12-800 (Washington, D.C.: July 12, 2012); and *Personnel Security Clearances: Continuing Leadership and Attention Can Enhance Momentum Gained from Reform Effort*, GAO-12-815T (Washington, D.C.: June 21, 2012).

[5]Security-clearance information from civilian agencies is maintained in OPM's Central Verification System (CVS). Security-clearance information from DOD employees and contractors is maintained in the Joint Personnel Adjudication System (JPAS). Security-clearance information from the intelligence community is maintained in the Scattered Castles database. CVS is capable of providing a bridge or link to JPAS security-clearance data, but the DOD data are not maintained in CVS. For our review, we did not study legislative-branch agencies in the OPM CVS database.

reinvestigation, from April 1, 2006, through December 31, 2011.[6] We used this time frame for the OPM Central Verification System (CVS) data because prior to April 1, 2006, the provision of the date a clearance was granted was not required and was therefore not consistently available for analysis. We electronically matched federal tax-debt data from the Internal Revenue Service (IRS) Unpaid Assessment database to these individuals using Social Security numbers (SSN). The OPM CVS database does not maintain information on the denial of security clearances on the basis of an individual's nonpayment of federal taxes. Thus, we were not able to determine the number of individuals who were denied security clearances for this reason. We included only those individuals with legally enforceable tax debts of $100 or more.[7] All individuals in the IRS tax-debt data had unpaid federal taxes as of June 30, 2012. The June 30, 2012, Unpaid Assessment file was used because it contained the most-recent unpaid-assessment information at the time we conducted our analysis. We assessed the reliability of the OPM data by performing electronic testing on the data and interviewing OPM officials regarding the quality and accuracy of the data. To assess the reliability of IRS unpaid-assessments data, we relied on the work we performed during our annual audit of the IRS's financial statements and discussions with the audit team. We also interviewed knowledgeable IRS officials about any data-reliability issues.[8] We determined that both the OPM and IRS data were sufficiently reliable to identify the individuals eligible for clearances with unpaid federal tax debt, provide an approximate overall amount of tax debt owed by these individuals, and select our case studies. Our final estimate of tax debt does include some debt that is covered under an active IRS installment plan or is beyond normal statutory time limits for debt collection. Our analysis determined the magnitude of known unpaid federal taxes owed by selected individuals in the OPM database and cannot be generalized to individuals

---

[6]Our review did not include the review of confidential clearance holders or public-trust positions. Department of Energy (DOE) and U.S. Nuclear Regulatory Commission (NRC) "Q" and "L" clearances are equivalent to the top-secret and secret clearances. Thus, for the purposes of our report, we considered "Q" and "L" clearances issued by DOE and NRC to be treated as top-secret and secret clearances, respectively.

[7]This threshold is defined by the IRS as a de minimis amount, below which any amount is so small as to make accounting for it unreasonable or impractical.

[8]See: GAO, *Financial Audit: IRS's Financial Audit Fiscal Years 2012 and 2011 Financial Statements*, GAO-13-120 (Washington, D.C.: Nov. 9, 2012).

that were granted eligibility for security clearances by DOD, the legislative branch, or the intelligence community.

To determine to what extent federal agencies have mechanisms to detect unpaid tax debt during the security-clearance approval process, we held meetings with knowledgeable officials from OPM, ODNI, the IRS, Department of Homeland Security (DHS), Department of Energy (DOE) and Department of State (State). We selected DHS, DOE, and State because these agencies had the highest number of security clearances, collectively representing over 50 percent of clearances granted in OPM's CVS database, and also represented over 50 percent of the tax debt owed. OPM conducts security-clearance investigations for most federal agencies. ODNI serves as Security Executive Agent for the federal government and has authority and responsibility over many aspects of the security-clearance program. As such, we also reviewed and analyzed applicable laws, regulations, and ODNI guidance, as well as applicable policies and procedures for OPM, DHS, DOE, and State regarding the investigation and adjudication of security clearances.[9] Finally, we conducted interviews with the Department of the Treasury's Bureau of the Fiscal Service (Fiscal Service) and the IRS on any initiatives and challenges in sharing tax debt information. We compared verification mechanisms with the fraud control framework we developed in our past work and other fraud-control best practices.[10] We also used Federal Investigative Standards (see app. I) and the Revised Adjudicative Guidelines for Determining Eligibility for Access to Classified Information (see app. II) to evaluate the current mechanisms used to identify and evaluate unpaid federal tax debt as part of the security-clearance process.

---

[9]A review of materials provided by OPM and ODNI, as well as federal regulations, provided an outline of the security-clearance process for the overall federal government. A review of materials provided by DOE, DHS, and State provided an outline of specific security-clearance processes employed by each agency.

[10]The fraud-prevention framework was developed on the basis of findings from GAO audits of Hurricanes Katrina and Rita relief efforts, and the internal control standards from the Standards for Internal Control in the Federal Government. For more detail, see GAO, *Hurricanes Katrina and Rita Disaster Relief: Prevention Is the Key to Minimizing Fraud, Waste, and Abuse in Recovery Efforts*, GAO-07-418T (Washington, D.C.: Jan. 29, 2007); GAO, *Government Operations: Standards for Internal Control in the Federal Government*, GAO/AIMD-00-21.3.1 (Washington, D.C.: Nov. 1, 1999), and the Committee of Sponsoring Organizations of the Treadway Commission (COSO), *Internal Control—Integrated Framework*.

To develop case-study examples, we identified a nonprobability sample of 13 individuals for detailed reviews from the above analyses of security-clearance holders from DHS, DOE, and State who had federal tax debt. These three agencies were selected because they had the largest number of individuals who were adjudicated as eligible for a security clearance from April 1, 2006, to December 31, 2011. We stratified our data matches using the following characteristics: (1) adjudicating agency; (2) amounts of unpaid federal taxes in the IRS Unpaid Assessment database as of June 30, 2012; (3) type of security clearance granted or approved, clearance date, and dollar amount of unpaid tax debt; and (4) whether tax debt was recorded prior to or after the security-clearance grant date. We then randomly selected 12 cases on the basis of these criteria. Additionally, we randomly selected one individual for whom IRS records show the taxpayer was assessed a penalty. We requested and obtained IRS notes, detailed account transcripts, and other records from the IRS as well as background investigation and adjudicative record files from DHS, DOE, and State for these 13 individuals. For 11 of the 13 individuals that had accrued debt before the adjudication, we reviewed the background investigation and adjudicative record files and IRS paperwork to determine whether the tax debt was revealed during the investigative or adjudicative processes, and, if so, how it was handled during the adjudication. For 2 of the 13 individuals that had accrued debt only after favorable adjudication, we reviewed the adjudicative files to determine whether the agency was aware of the federal tax debt through its reinvestigation. These cases were selected to illustrate individuals with unpaid federal tax debt that had been determined eligible for security clearances but cannot be generalized beyond the cases presented. A more-detailed description of the scope and methodology can be found in appendix III.

We conducted this performance audit from November 2011 to September 2013 in accordance with generally accepted government auditing standards. Those standards require that we plan and perform the audit to obtain sufficient, appropriate evidence to provide a reasonable basis for our audit findings and conclusions based on our audit objectives. We believe that the evidence obtained provides a reasonable basis for our findings and conclusions based on our audit objectives.

Background

Unpaid Federal Tax Debt Owed

As of September 30, 2012, the tax debt of individuals and businesses that owed the U.S. government was about $364 billion, according to the IRS.[11] The tax-debt inventory is the sum of all taxes owed to the IRS at a particular point in time, including debts from the current year and debts from previous years that fall within the 10-year statute of limitations on collections. The inventory of tax debts comprises tax assessments that are not collected along with related penalty and interest charges. Federal taxes that are owed become tax debts when the tax is assessed but not paid. Millions of individual and business taxpayers owe billions of dollars in unpaid federal tax debts, and the IRS expends substantial resources trying to collect these debts.

Given the many challenges that the IRS faces in the enforcement of U.S. tax laws, this area continues to be on our list of high-risk areas.[12] We have previously reported that many individuals with tax debt take advantage of government programs, such as federal contracts, grants, Medicare, Medicaid, and loan insurance, thereby reaping benefits from these programs while failing to pay their own taxes.[13] In addition, the IRS issues an annual report on the Federal Employee/Retiree Delinquency Initiative (FERDI) to promote federal tax compliance among current and retired federal employees.[14] The most-recent report states that federal employees represented about 3 percent of all delinquent taxpayers in the

---

[11]The tax debt inventory contains known unpaid taxes, penalties, and interest, see GAO, *Federal Tax Debts: Factors for Considering a Proposal to Report Tax Debts to Credit Bureaus.* GAO-12-939 (Washington, D.C.: Sept. 10, 2012). This figure includes all U.S. taxpayers, including federal employees and federal contractors.

[12]GAO, *High-Risk Series: An Update*, GAO-13-283 (Washington, D.C.: February 2013).

[13]See Related GAO Products section at the end of this report for a listing of our previous work in this area.

[14]The annual report includes civilian employees of the executive, legislative, and judicial branches, U.S. Postal Service employees, civilian retirees, active-duty military, National Guard and reservist personnel, as well as military retirees.

workforce (approximately 312,000 individuals).[15] The report does not contain a comparison of the delinquency rates of federal employees with the general population.

Laws and Regulations Governing the Security-Clearance Process

Passed in 2004, the Intelligence Reform and Terrorism Prevention Act (IRTPA) mandates the President to identify a single entity responsible for, among other things, directing the day-to-day oversight of investigations and adjudications for personnel security clearances throughout the U.S. government.[16] Additionally, agencies may not establish additional investigative or adjudicative requirements without approval from the selected entity, nor may they conduct an investigation where an investigation or adjudicative determination of equal level exists.[17]

Executive Order 13467 (June 30, 2008) designates ODNI as the Security Executive Agent and assigns responsibility for developing uniform and consistent policies and procedures to ensure the effective, efficient, and timely completion of investigations and adjudications related to determinations of eligibility for access to classified information or eligibility to hold a sensitive position. Executive Order 13467 also designates the Director of OPM as the Suitability Executive Agent responsible for developing and implementing uniform and consistent policies and procedures for investigations and adjudications related to determinations of suitability for federal employment, as well as eligibility for electronic and

---

[15]According to the IRS, an employee is considered delinquent if he or she has an unresolved federal income-tax delinquency in the form of a balance owed or an unfiled tax return, or both. Accounts in the status of currently not collectble, combat zone, offer in compromise, or bankruptcy/litigation are included in the analysis. Federal employees in repayment plans are excluded.

[16]Pub. L. No. 108-458, § 3001 (Dec. 17, 2004).

[17]Pursuant to IRTPA, the Office of Management and Budget designated OPM as the single agency of the executive branch to conduct, to the maximum extent practicable, security-clearance investigations. According to OPM officials, OPM conducts background investigations for DOD, including for defense contract employment and military service; OPM conducts personnel security, suitability, and qualifications-related investigations for employment in the competitive civil service. Individual agencies are responsible for conducting investigations for excepted service and contract employment that does not require clearances, but they may utilize OPM for this purpose.

physical access to secure facilities.[18] Additionally, Executive Order 13467 outlines a process for continuous evaluation of individuals that are determined to be eligible or currently have access to classified information. Continuous evaluation means reviewing the background of an individual who has been determined to be eligible for access to classified information (including additional or new checks of commercial databases, government databases, and other information lawfully available to security officials) at any time during the period of eligibility to determine whether that individual continues to meet the requirements for eligibility for access to classified information. Executive Order 12968 (August 4, 1995) authorized establishment of uniform security policies, procedures, and practices, including the Federal Investigative Standards used by investigators conducting security-clearance investigations. In December 2012, the Security and Suitability Executive Agents (ODNI and OPM) jointly issued a revised version of Federal Investigative Standards for the conduct of background investigations for individuals that work for or on behalf of the federal government.

Security-Clearance Process

Personnel security clearances are required for access to classified national-security information, which may be classified at one of three levels: confidential, secret, or top secret. A top-secret clearance is generally also required for access to Sensitive Compartmented Information or Special Access Programs.[19] The level of classification denotes the degree of protection required for information and the amount of damage that unauthorized disclosure could reasonably be expected to cause to national security. Unauthorized disclosure could reasonably be expected to cause (1) "damage," in the case of confidential information; (2) "serious damage," in the case of secret information; and (3) "exceptionally grave damage," in the case of top-secret information.[20]

---

[18]The executive branch uses suitability determinations to ensure individuals are suitable, on the basis of character and conduct, for federal employment in certain positions. Suitability determinations are separate from security-clearance determinations that are used for access to national-security information.

[19] Sensitive Compartmented Information relates to positions that require access to unique or uniquely productive intelligence sources or methods vital to the U.S. security.

[20]Exec. Order No. 13526, 75 Fed. Reg. 707 (Dec. 29, 2009).

As shown in figure 1, to ensure the trustworthiness and reliability of personnel in positions with access to classified information, government agencies rely on a personnel security-clearance process that includes multiple phases: application, investigation, adjudication, and reinvestigation (where applicable, for renewal or upgrade of an existing clearance).

Figure 1: Overview of the Federal Security-Clearance Process

Phase 1: Application

Suitability initial screening
Applicant completes suitability process for federal employment (includes submission of Optional Form 306).

Reciprocity determination
Requesting agency checks personnel security databases to determine whether an existing investigation or adjudication meets current requirements.

Office of Personnel Management (OPM) Standard Form 86 (SF-86)
SF-86 completed by applicant and submitted to requesting agency via Electronic Questionnaires for Investigations Processing. Agency reviews application for completeness and accuracy based on OPM requirements. Application submitted to OPM or other designated provider for investigation.

Phase 2: Investigation

OPM background investigation
OPM performs background investigation following Federal Investigative Standards. SF-86 and credit report reviewed, and applicant may be interviewed (for top secret or to clarify information). To verify financial information on a case-by-case basis, OPM may obtain an Internal Revenue Service (IRS) disclosure waiver from the applicant to request IRS tax records for specified tax years.

Phase 3: Adjudication

Agency adjudication
Agency adjudicator reviews the investigative report for suitability and National Security concerns. Security clearance determination is based on "whole person" concept applied across 13 Federal Adjudicative Guidelines. Applicant may submit evidence to clarify information. Applicant notified of final determination and is entitled to appeals process for denials, suspensions, and revocations.

Ongoing monitoring
Agencies may perform ongoing monitoring per terms of conditional clearance status.

Phase 4: Reinvestigation

Renewal
Reinvestigation covers the period from time of previous clearance grant date to date of new application. Renewal of clearance at the same level occurs every 10 years for secret or 5 years for top secret.

Upgrade
Applicants for upgrade of clearance undergo additional steps necessary to obtain the higher clearance level (such as subject interview for top secret).

Source: GAO analysis based on Office of the Director of National Intelligence, Office of Personnel Management, and selected agencies data. Art Explosion (images).

Note: Data are from agencies' clearance-processing protocols and this process does not apply to agencies in the intelligence community.

GAO-13-733 Security Clearances and Federal Tax Debt

The application phase. To determine whether an investigation would be required, the agency requesting a security-clearance investigation is to first conduct a check of existing personnel-security databases to determine whether there is an existing security-clearance investigation underway or whether the individual has already been favorably adjudicated for a clearance in accordance with current standards. If such a security clearance does not exist for that individual, a security officer from an agency is to (1) request an investigation of an individual requiring a clearance; (2) forward a personnel-security questionnaire (SF-86) to the individual to complete using OPM's Electronic Questionnaires for Investigations Processing (e-QIP) system; (3) review the completed questionnaire; and (4) send the questionnaire and supporting documentation, such as fingerprints, to OPM or another designated investigative service provider.[21]

The investigation phase. OPM conducts a majority of the government's background investigations; however, some agencies, such as State, are delegated to conduct their own background investigations. Federal investigative standards and agencies' internal guidance are used to conduct and document the investigation of the applicant (see app. II). The scope of information gathered during an investigation depends on the level of clearance needed. For example, federal standards require that investigators collect information from national agencies, such as the Federal Bureau of Investigation, for all initial and renewal clearances. For an investigation for a confidential or secret clearance, investigators gather much of the information electronically. For an investigation for a top-secret clearance, investigators gather additional information through more-time-consuming efforts, such as traveling to conduct in-person interviews to corroborate information about an applicant's employment and education. After the investigation is complete, the resulting investigative report is provided to the agency.

The adjudication phase. Adjudicators from an agency use the information from the investigative report to determine whether an applicant is eligible for a security clearance. To make clearance-eligibility decisions, national policy requires adjudicators to consider the information against the 2005 Revised Adjudicative Guidelines for Determining

---

[21]The e-QIP system is a web-based automated system that was designed to facilitate the processing of standard investigative forms used when conducting background investigations for federal security, suitability, fitness, and credentialing purposes.

Eligibility for Access to Classified Information. The adjudication process is a careful weighing of a number of variables, to include disqualifying and mitigating factors, known as the "whole-person" concept. When a person's life history shows evidence of unreliability or untrustworthiness, questions can arise as to whether the person can be relied on and trusted to exercise the responsibility necessary for working in a secure environment where protecting national security is paramount. As part of the adjudication process, the adjudicative guidelines require agencies to determine whether a prospective individual meets the adjudicative criteria for determining eligibility, including personal conduct and financial considerations. If an individual has conditions that raise a security concern or may be disqualifying, the adjudicator must evaluate whether there are other factors that mitigate such risks (such as a good-faith effort to repay a federal tax debt). On the basis of this assessment, the agency may make a risk-management decision to grant the security-clearance eligibility determination, possibly with a warning that future incidents of a similar nature may result in revocation of access.

The reinvestigation phase. Personnel cleared for access to classified information may have their clearance renewed or upgraded if determined necessary to the performance of job requirements. Reinvestigation covers the period since the previous investigation. Renewal of a clearance at the same level currently undergoes the above process every 10 years for secret or 5 years for top secret.[22] Applicants for clearance upgrades undergo additional steps necessary to obtain the higher clearance level (such as a subject interview for a top-secret clearance).

Improvements to the Federal Security-Clearance Process

We have previously reported on issues related to the federal security-clearance process. For example, in 2005, we designated DOD's personnel security-clearance program—which comprises the vast majority of government wide clearances—as a high-risk area. This designation continued through 2011 because of concerns regarding continued delays in the clearance process and security-clearance documentation, among other things.[23] Since we first identified the DOD personnel security-clearance program as a high-risk area, DOD, in

---

[22]Once implemented, the revised Federal Investigative Standards approved in December 2012 will require 5-year reinvestigations for all clearances.

[23]GAO-12-815T.

conjunction with Congress and executive-agency leadership, took actions that resulted in significant progress toward improving the processing of security clearances. Congress held more than 14 oversight hearings to help oversee key legislation, such as the Intelligence Reform and Terrorism Prevention Act of 2004 (IRTPA), which helped focus attention and sustain momentum of the government-wide reform effort. In 2011, we removed DOD's personnel-security clearance program from our high-risk list because of the agency's progress in improving timeliness, development of tools and metrics to assess quality, and commitment to sustaining progress.

In 2012, we found that OPM's reported costs to conduct background investigations increased by about 80 percent, from about $600 million in fiscal year 2005 to almost $1.1 billion in 2011 (in fiscal year 2011 dollars).[24] OPM's background investigation program has several cost drivers, including investigation fieldwork and personnel compensation for OPM's background-investigation federal workforce. OPM attributed cost increases to, in part, an increase in the number of top-secret clearance investigations, which involve additional field work and more comprehensive subject interviews and compliance with investigation timeliness requirements.

---

[24]See GAO, *Background Investigations: Office of Personnel Management Needs to Improve Transparency of Its Pricing and Seek Cost Savings*, GAO-12-197 (Washington, D.C.: Feb. 28, 2012).

More Than 8,000 Individuals Eligible for Security Clearances Owe about $85 Million in Federal Taxes; About Half Are on Payment Plans with the IRS

About 240,000 employees and contractors of civilian executive-branch agencies, excluding known employees and contractors of DOD and intelligence agencies, had a federal security clearance or were approved for secret and top-secret clearances due to a favorable adjudication from April 1, 2006, through December 31, 2011.[25] These consist of both initial investigations when an individual is applying for a clearance and reinvestigations when an individual is upgrading to a higher clearance level or renewing an existing clearance. About 8,400 of the 240,000 people (approximately 3.5 percent) had unpaid federal tax debt as of June 30, 2012, totaling about $85 million. The characteristics and nature of these 8,400 individuals with tax debt are discussed below.

- **About half of the individuals are in a repayment plan with the IRS.** According to IRS data, about 4,200 of these 8,400 individuals with tax debt had a repayment plan with the IRS to pay back their debt as of June 30, 2012.[26] The tax debt owed by those on a repayment plan was approximately $35 million.
- **About half of individuals with tax debt were federal employees.** About 4,700 of the approximately 8,400 individuals with tax debt were federal employees, while the remainder were employees of federal contractors or had an "other" designation used to identify other categories of individuals.[27]
- **About half of the individuals with tax debt were eligible for a top-secret clearance.** About 4,200 of these 8,400 individuals were favorably adjudicated as eligible for a top-secret clearance during our

---

[25]There were approximately 280,000 unique clearances in the OPM CVS database. These numbers exclude DOD, legislative-branch, and intelligence-agency employees. About 240,000 individuals held or were approved for these 280,000 clearances. Our review did not include the review of confidential clearance holders or public-trust positions. DOE and NRC "Q" and "L" clearances are equivalent to the top-secret and secret clearances. Thus, for the purposes of our report, we considered "Q" and "L" clearances issued by DOE and NRC to be treated as top-secret and secret clearances, respectively.

[26]Repayment plans, or installment agreements, are monthly payments made to the IRS that allow individuals or entities to repay their federal tax debt over an extended period.

[27]According to ODNI, the "other" category consists of individuals who held or were approved for security clearances but could not be categorized as either a federal employee or a contractor. Therefore, all CVS data that could not be categorized by employee type are captured in this category.

time frame (April 1, 2006, to December 31, 2011), while the others were favorably adjudicated as eligible for a secret clearance.[28]

- **Most individuals accrued tax debt after clearance adjudication.** Approximately 6,300 individuals (about 76 percent) accrued tax debts only after the issuance of the security clearance. Approximately 2,000 individuals (about 25 percent) accrued their tax debt before the approval for the security clearance.
- **Age and amount of tax debt ranges widely.** About 16 percent of the $85 million in unpaid federal taxes were delinquent more than 3 years, and approximately 6 percent of the unpaid federal taxes were delinquent more than 5 years. Further, the unpaid tax debt of each individual ranged from approximately $100 to over $2 million, and the median tax-debt amount owed by these individuals was approximately $3,800.

In addition, we analyzed 13 nongeneralizable case examples—7 federal contractors and 6 federal employees from the DOE, DHS, and State—to determine whether existing investigative and adjudication mechanisms detected unpaid tax debt during the security-clearance process. In 8 of these 13 cases, the individual had a top-secret clearance, with the remaining 5 having secret clearances. In 5 of the 13 cases, the individual had a reinvestigation of the security clearance after the period of our analysis (April 1, 2006, to December 31, 2011). In 11 of these 13 cases, the individual's tax debt accrued before the favorable adjudication of the security clearance. For all 11 of these cases, the tax debt was identified either through the initial investigation or through the reinvestigation. In 2 of the 13 cases, the individual's tax debt accrued after the favorable adjudication of the security clearance, and no indication of the federal tax debt was found in the security clearance files. On the basis of our review of IRS records, our analysis found that 12 of the 13 individuals filed their tax returns late for at least 1 tax year, and 6 of the 13 individuals did not file at least one annual tax return.[29] These specific case studies are discussed throughout the report.

---

[28]Certain individuals may have both top-secret and secret clearances during this period. ODNI, *2012 Report on Security Clearance Determinations* (January 2013).

[29]The IRS database does not reflect amounts owed by businesses and individuals that have not filed tax returns and for which the IRS has not assessed tax amounts due. Our analysis did not attempt to account for businesses or individuals that underreported taxes owed or were not specifically identified by the IRS as owing additional federal taxes.

Federal Agencies Have Mechanisms to Detect Tax Debt, but Opportunities Exist to Strengthen Detection Capabilities

To detect federal tax debt for clearance applicants, consistent with federal law, federal investigators rely primarily on two methods: (1) applicants self-reporting tax debts, and (2) validation techniques, such as the use of credit reports or in-person interviews. Each of these methods has shortcomings in detecting unpaid federal tax debts for clearance applicants. Moreover, federal agencies do not routinely monitor individuals after the security clearance is favorably adjudicated to identify tax debt accrued subsequent to the clearance approval. Additional mechanisms that provide large-scale, routine detection of federal tax debt could improve federal agencies' ability to detect tax debts owed by security-clearance applicants and current clearance holders.

Investigation Mechanisms Include Self-Reporting and Validation Techniques

Self-Reporting

As part of the application-submission phase of the security-clearance process, applicants must submit various background and biographical information using OPM form SF-86. In addition, new federal employees typically complete the Declaration for Federal Employment form (OF-306). Both of these forms require applicants to disclose if they are delinquent on any federal debt, including tax debts. The SF-86 is used in conducting background investigations, reinvestigations, and continuous evaluations of federal employees and contractors. The SF-86 requires that applicants declare if they did not file or pay any federal taxes within the past 7 years. The SF-86 also requires applicants to disclose whether any liens were placed on their property for failure to pay tax debts and whether they are currently delinquent on any federal debts (including tax debts). Similar to the SF-86, the Declaration for Federal Employment requires applicants to disclose if they are delinquent on any federal debt, including tax debts. If the applicant is delinquent, the applicant is required to disclose, among other things, the type and amount of debt and any steps taken to repay the debt. An excerpt of the SF-86 where applicants are required to disclose any tax issues are illustrated in figure 2.

Figure 2: Excerpt of Office of Personnel Management (OPM) Form SF-86

26.3 **In the past seven (7) years** have you failed to file or pay Federal, state, or other taxes when required by law or ordinance?   ☐ YES   ☐ NO *(If NO, proceed to 26.4)*

Complete the following if you responded **'Yes'** to having failed to file or pay Federal, state, or other taxes when required by law or ordinance.

Entry #1

Did you fail to file, pay as required, or both?
☐ File   ☐ Pay   ☐ Both

Provide the year you failed to file or pay your Federal, state, or other taxes.
☐ Est.

Provide the reason(s) for your failure to file or pay required taxes.

Provide the Federal, state, or other agency to which you failed to file or pay taxes.

Provide the type of taxes you failed to file or pay (such as property, income, sales, etc.).

Provide the amount (in U.S. dollars) of the taxes. ☐ Est.

Provide date satisfied. *(Month/Year)*

☐ Not Applicable   ☐ Est.

Provide a description of any action(s) you have taken to satisfy this debt (such as withholdings, frequency and amount of payments, etc.). If you have not taken any action(s) provide explanation.

Entry #2

Did you fail to file, pay as required, or both?
☐ File   ☐ Pay   ☐ Both

Provide the year you failed to file or pay your Federal, state, or other taxes.
☐ Est.

Provide the reason(s) for your failure to file or pay required taxes.

Provide the Federal, state, or other agency to which you failed to file or pay taxes.

Provide the type of taxes you failed to file or pay (such as property, income, sales, etc.).

Provide the amount (in U.S. dollars) of the taxes. ☐ Est.

Provide date satisfied. *(Month/Year)*

☐ Not Applicable   ☐ Est.

Provide a description of any action(s) you have taken to satisfy this debt (such as withholdings, frequency and amount of payments, etc.). If you have not taken any action(s) provide explanation.

Source: OPM.

Of the 13 individuals we examined from our nongeneralizable sample, 11 had accrued debt prior to the clearance being granted. Our review of the SF-86 documentation for this sample of 11 selected cases found that 5 individuals did not properly disclose their tax debts. Each of these individuals owed at least $12,000 at the time of our review. As discussed later in this report, our past work has focused on the inadequacies of relying on self-reported information without independent verification and review.

Validation Techniques

During the investigative phase, the investigative agency can perform several activities in an effort to validate applicants' certifications about the nature and extent of their tax debts, but each of the techniques has limitations, as discussed below.

Obtaining credit reports of the applicants. According to OPM officials, credit reports, which contain public records including federal tax liens, are the primary method of identifying federal tax debts that were not self-reported.[30] However, credit reports only contain information on tax debts for which the IRS filed a lien on the debtor's property, both real and personal, for the amount of the unpaid tax. Circumstances do not warrant a lien being filed in all cases, such as when the amount of the debt is in dispute or when the IRS determines that filing a lien would hamper collection of the debt because the debtor is trying to obtain a loan to pay it off.[31] In addition, the IRS generally does not file liens until after the debt has moved out of the notice status and there is property on which a lien can be placed.[32] The amount owed can increase with interest and penalties or can decrease as the debtor makes payments, but neither change is reflected in the recorded tax lien amount. Our analysis found that about 450 of the approximately 8,400 delinquent taxpayers (about 5 percent) who were favorably adjudicated as eligible for security clearances had a tax lien filed on them. For the 13 cases that we reviewed, 4 of the cases identified during the investigative process had tax liens filed against the individuals.

---

[30]If a tax debtor does not pay after the IRS's initial contact to collect an assessed tax debt, the IRS has the authority to protect the government's interests by filing a Notice of Federal Tax Lien. A taxpayer must be given notice and an opportunity for a hearing when a federal tax lien is filed. Such a lien attaches a claim to all of the debtor's property, both real and personal, for the amount of unpaid tax, including any interest and penalties. Unlike the IRS's authority to levy or seize assets, a lien does not authorize the IRS to take possession of an asset or deprive the taxpayer of use of an asset. Instead, a lien publicly records the debt owed by the taxpayer as a notice to possible future creditors and to establish priority rights against certain other creditors that may also hold liens or secured rights against a taxpayer's assets.

[31]For cases in which the IRS has not filed a lien, the government's interest in the tax debtor's property is not protected.

[32]The IRS has a complex process to attempt the collection of tax debts. As a first stage, the IRS sends a series of notices to notify the debtor of the debt owed and to prompt payment or other debtor response, such as to dispute the debt or request to enter into an installment payment agreement. If the debt is not resolved by notices, the IRS may then initiate contact with the taxpayer by telephone or in person. After the notice phase, the IRS can also take enforcement action, such as placing liens, or levying or seizing assets.

Conducting in-person interviews. As part of the investigation, investigators may conduct interviews with the applicant and his or her friends, former spouses, neighbors, and other individuals associated with the applicant. According to OPM, during the course of the in-person interviews, the tax debt could be disclosed, but there is no systematic way to identify tax debt during the interviews. For example, according to State officials, state tax debt is usually an indicator that the individual also owes federal taxes. Thus, during the course of their in-person interviews, investigators will often inquire with the applicant whether he or she owes federal taxes when a state tax debt is discovered. However the in-person interviews can be a time-consuming and resource-intensive process, and OPM does not have assurance that it identifies all tax debt information through the interview process.

Agencies Do Not Routinely Monitor Current Clearance Holders for Tax Debt

Federal agencies generally do not have routine mechanisms to review federal tax compliance for individuals who hold security clearances. Specifically, there is no process to detect unpaid federal tax debts accrued after an individual has been favorably adjudicated as eligible for a security clearance unless it is self-reported, reported by a security manager due to garnishment of wages, or discovered during a clearance reinvestigation (renewal) or upgrade. Given that individuals who hold security clearances are reinvestigated every 10 years for secret clearances and every 5 years for top-secret clearances, if an individual accrues tax debt after a security clearance is granted, the unpaid federal tax debt may not be detected for up to 5-10 years. As previously discussed, in 2 of our 13 case studies, the individuals' tax debt accrued after the favorable adjudication of the security clearance, and we found no indication that the federal tax debt was identified in the security-clearance file. In addition, if the tax debt is not found in the initial investigation, the federal agency may not detect the tax debt until the next security clearance reinvestigation. In 5 of the cases that we reviewed, existing federal tax debt was not identified in the original adjudication of the security clearance but through the subsequent reinvestigation of the security clearance, meaning the individuals had tax debt unknown to the federal agency while holding a clearance for some period of time. This gap represents a risk that could be mitigated by a mechanism to routinely obtain tax-debt information, as discussed later in this report.

Example 3: Individual Accruing Federal Tax Debt after Being Granted a Security Clearance

A federal employee was approved for a top-secret clearance in the late 2000s. After the clearance was approved, the employee accrued over $10,000 of federal tax debt. Agency adjudicators were not aware of this tax debt at the time of our review.

Source: GAO analysis of agency and IRS records.

Opportunities Exist to Improve Detection of Tax Debt Owed by Security-Clearance Applicants and Clearance Holders

Additional mechanisms that provide large-scale detection of federal tax debt could improve federal agencies' ability to detect tax debts owed by security-clearance applicants and security-clearance holders, but statutory privacy protections limit access to this information. Specifically, access to the federal tax information needed to obtain the tax payment status of applicants is restricted under section 6103 of the Internal Revenue Code, which generally prohibits disclosure of taxpayer data to federal agencies and others, including disclosures to help validate an applicant's certifications about the nature and extent of his or her tax debt.[33] During our interviews, ODNI, DHS, DOE, and State officials expressed interest in establishing additional mechanisms to provide large-scale detection of unpaid tax debt owed by security-clearance applicants. ODNI officials stated that they formed a working group in 2012, in collaboration with OPM and other federal agencies, to, among other things, explore whether an automated process for reviewing federal tax compliance can be established.[34] However, restrictions to taxpayer information under section 6103 may present challenges to their efforts. For example, in 2011 and 2012, State requested the IRS to provide it a listing of State employees who owed federal taxes. The IRS did not formally respond in writing to the State letters, according to State officials, but stated that the IRS could not provide them this list due to section 6103 restrictions. According to IRS officials, based on their analysis of the applicable tax laws, IRS cannot disclose tax information of federal employees without taxpayer consent request.

Federal agencies may obtain information on federal tax debts directly from the IRS if the applicant provides consent. For example, agencies can use IRS form 4506-T, Request for Transcript of Tax Return, to obtain tax transcripts that provide basic taxpayer information, including marital status, type of return filed, adjusted gross income, taxable income, and later adjustments, if any, if the individual provides written consent. However, this form may not be useful in conducting routine checks with the IRS during the initial investigation and reinvestigation processes for three reasons. First, the use of the IRS form 4506-T is a manual process and thus it is not conducive to the large-scale detection of unpaid federal taxes owed by security-clearance applicants, according to OPM, DHS, and State officials. Instead, this method is typically performed when a

---

[33]26 U.S.C. § 6103.

[34]ODNI officials stated that they do not have a time frame for the completion of their work.

federal tax debt is disclosed by the applicant or discovered during the investigation. Second, the IRS form 4506-T generally provides limited visibility into an applicant's overall tax debt status because the form requires the requesting agency to identify the specific tax modules (generally, time periods) that the agencies are requesting to be disclosed, and, as such, agencies may not obtain the complete tax debt history of the individual. Finally, the IRS form 4506-T has a 120-day time limit from date of the applicant's signature providing consent to process the form with the IRS. Officials from State stated that this limited time frame could hinder their ability to obtain the requested tax information if this form was provided at the time the security-clearance application was completed. As highlighted in our past work, it is important that the establishment of any federal tax-compliance check not delay the timeliness of security-clearance decisions. Specifically, timeliness concerns were one of the reasons that we designated the security-clearance process as high risk from 2005 to 2011.[35] As we concluded in July 2012, delays in the security-clearance process could pose risks to national security, impede the start of classified work and hiring the best-qualified workers, and increase the government's cost of national-security-related contracts.[36]

The Department of the Treasury's Offset Program (TOP), or a similar mechanism, may provide an opportunity for federal agencies to perform an automated check of both security-clearance applicants and current clearance holders to determine whether they have unpaid federal debts that would include tax debts, while not violating IRS section 6103 requirements.[37] TOP is an automated process administered by the Department of the Treasury in which certain federal payments, such as contractor and federal salary payments, are reduced to collect certain delinquent tax and nontax debts owed to federal agencies, including the

---

[35]GAO, *High-Risk Series: An Update*, GAO-11-278 (Washington, D.C.: Feb. 16, 2011).

[36]GAO-12-800.

[37]The Federal Payment Levy Program (FPLP) is the continuous levy program that uses TOP to levy federal payments against federal tax debts. In 2011, the IRS reported that it collected over $600 million through FPLP.

IRS.[38] Each week, the IRS sends the Department of the Treasury's Bureau of the Fiscal Service office (Fiscal Service) an extract of its tax-debt files, which are uploaded into TOP and matched against Fiscal Service payment data (such as federal contractor payments, federal salary payments, and Social Security Administration retirement payments). If there is a match and the IRS has completed all statutory notifications, any federal payment owed to the debtor is reduced (levied) to help satisfy the unpaid federal taxes.[39]

As we concluded in our past work, since TOP comingles information regarding tax debt and nontax debt, the existence of an employee's name in TOP would generally not be considered taxpayer information subject to section 6103 of the tax code.[40] Thus, TOP could be used to identify individuals who may owe federal debts, which includes federal taxes, without compromising privacy protections provided by section 6103. TOP currently reports a federal debt indicator (comprising both federal tax and nontax debts) to the System for Award Management (SAM) on whether a federal contractor or grant recipient has federal debts.[41] SAM is a

---

[38]Payment agencies prepare and certify payment vouchers to the Bureau of the Fiscal Service (Fiscal Service) and disbursing officials at other federal agencies that are non–Department of the Treasury–disbursed, who then disburse payments. The payment vouchers contain information about the payment, including the name and Tax Identification Number (TIN) of the recipient. Before an eligible federal payment is disbursed to a payee, disbursing officials compare the payment information with debtor information, which has been supplied by the creditor agency, in the Fiscal Service delinquent-debtor database. If the payee's name and TIN match the name and TIN of a debtor, the disbursing official offsets the payment, in whole or in part, to satisfy the debt, to the extent legally allowed. The TOP also has state debts that payments may offset. These state debts include certain child-support debts, tax debts, and unemployment-insurance compensation debts.

[39]For more information on TOP process for tax debts, see GAO, *Financial Management: Thousands of Civilian Agency Contractors Abuse the Federal Tax System with Little Consequence,* GAO-05-637 (Washington, D.C.: June, 2005).

[40]GAO, *Taxpayer Confidentiality: Federal, State, and Local Agencies Receiving Taxpayer Information,* GAO/GGD-99-164 (Washington, D.C.: Aug. 30, 1999).

[41]Federal agencies are required to review this field when they are making federal payments to the contractor or grant recipient. If a federal agency finds that a contractor owes federal debt, the federal agency should pay the contractor through the disbursing office, and not an agency purchase card, so that the federal payment can be offset or levied against the federal debt. The federal debt indicator does not distinguish between federal tax debt and federal nontax debt. As such, there is not an unlawful disclosure of taxpayer information.

government-wide database used to track the status of agency procurements.

As of September 2012, the IRS had referred approximately $167 billion (approximately 44 percent) of the $373 billion of the total unpaid tax assessment inventory in tax debts to TOP; thus, this program is an important repository of tax-debt data for federal workers and contractors. The IRS typically sends the tax debts to TOP except in cases where

(1) the IRS has not completed its notification process,[42]

(2) tax debtors have filed for bankruptcy protection or other litigation,

(3) tax debtors have agreed to pay their tax debt through monthly installment payments or have requested to pay less than the full amount owed through an offer in compromise,

(4) the IRS determined that the tax debtors are in financial hardship,

(5) tax debtors are filing an amended return, or

(6) the IRS determined that specific circumstances (such as a criminal investigation) exist that warrant special exclusion from FPLP.[43]

Thus, debts that are typically sent to TOP are those where the taxpayer has not shown a willingness to resolve his or her tax debts. As such, it is important that these individuals are identified because it can be an important factor in determining whether an individual should be eligible for a security clearance, as inability or unwillingness to satisfy debts is a potentially disqualifying factor according to the adjudicative guidelines. Our analysis found that 1,600 (approximately 20 percent) of the 8,400 taxpayers that had been granted security clearances during this 5-year period had tax debts that were referred to TOP.

A mechanism similar to or using TOP could be useful in identifying individuals who have not shown a willingness to resolve their tax debts

---

[42]During this process, IRS sends a series of up to four separate notices to tax debtors demanding payment of their taxes. The IRS must send two notices—a Notice and Demand for Payment and a Final Notice of Intent to Levy—before the debts can be sent to TOP.

[43]For more details, see GAO, *Internal Revenue Service: Procedural Changes Could Enhance Tax Collections*, GAO-07-26 (Washington, D.C.: Nov. 15, 2006).

and who are applying for a security clearance or already have one.[44] This type of mechanism can be especially advantageous in monitoring clearance holders to identify circumstances (such as the nonpayment of federal taxes) that might warrant a reevaluation of an individual's security-clearance eligibility.[45] As discussed earlier, our analysis found that 6,375 individuals (approximately 76 percent) had their tax debt accrued after the approval for the security clearance.

While ODNI officials reported forming a working group with OPM and other federal agencies to explore an automated process for reviewing federal tax compliance, ODNI, IRS, and Fiscal Service officials stated that they have not explored the use of TOP for identifying individuals who owe federal debts, including tax debts.[46] ODNI officials stated that they would be supportive of processes that automatically checked security-clearance applicants for federal tax debts. Fiscal Service officials stated that they did not foresee any potential operational issues with using TOP more broadly for these purposes. However, IRS and Fiscal Service officials stated that a legal analysis would need to be performed to determine if the TOP information could be used for the purpose of performing background investigations.

Separate from TOP, agencies may determine that a change in law is required to access taxpayer information without having to get consent from the individual. If it is determined that a change in law would be required, the IRS and federal agencies could consider various factors in determining whether they should seek legislative action for disclosing taxpayer information as part of the security-clearance process. Specifically, as we concluded in December 2011, it is important that Congress consider both the benefits expected from a disclosure of federal tax information and the expected costs, including reduced taxpayer

Example 4: Security Clearance Holder Referred to Treasury Offset Program (TOP) for Tax Levy

A federal employee granted a secret clearance in the late 2000s owed thousands of dollars in federal taxes from the mid-to-late 2000s. The investigator discovered the unpaid federal taxes as part of the security-clearance process. The employee told investigators the debt was being resolved through a repayment plan. However, IRS records showed that the federal employee periodically defaulted on the repayment plan. As a result, the IRS referred the tax debts to TOP in the early 2010s so that any federal payments, including salary, would be levied to repay the tax debts. The tax debts were referred to TOP the same year the security clearance was granted.

Source: GAO analysis of agency and IRS records.

---

[44]Fiscal Service officials noted that a similar program "Do Not Pay" already exists for the purpose of identifying federal debt. However, this program does not contain federal tax debts.

[45]Executive Order 13467 (2008) amended Executive Order 12968 (1995) by inserting Section 3.5, which authorizes continuous evaluation of cleared personnel according to standards to be established by ODNI. These standards have not yet been implemented.

[46]In December 2012, ODNI and OPM jointly issued new investigative standards requiring tax-compliance checks as part of any security-clearance investigation or reinvestigation. OPM believes that this change will accommodate the addition of any new tax checks that are authorized.

privacy, risk of inappropriate disclosure, and negative effects on tax compliance and tax-system administration.[47]

While knowingly making false statements on federal security-clearance forms is a federal crime and may deter some from lying about their tax debt, much of our prior work has focused on the inadequacies of using voluntary, self-reported information without independent verification and review.[48] In our past work, we found that independent verification is a key detection and monitoring component of our agency's fraud-prevention framework and is a fraud-control best practice.[49] Routinely obtaining federal debt information from the Department of the Treasury would allow investigative agencies to conduct this independent validation.

In addition, as previously discussed, currently there is no method to monitor clearance holders to detect unpaid federal tax debts accrued after an individual has been favorably adjudicated as eligible for a security clearance, unless it is self-reported, reported by a security manager due to garnishment of wages, or discovered during a clearance reinvestigation. This is especially important as about 76 percent of the individuals in our review accrued tax debts only after the issuance of the security clearance. While security-clearance investigators identified tax debt in the majority of our case studies, in some cases they did not identify the debt in the course of the initial clearance investigation, but during the subsequent reinvestigation. Given that clearance holders are only subject to reinvestigations every 5-10 years, an automated mechanism would allow federal agencies to routinely monitor clearance

---

[47]GAO, *Taxpayer Privacy: A Guide for Screening and Assessing Proposals to Disclose Confidential Tax Information to Specific Parties for Specific Purposes*, GAO-12-231SP (Washington, D.C.: Dec. 14, 2011).

[48]See, for example, GAO, *Recovery Act Tax Debtors Have Received FHA Mortgage Insurance and First-Time Homebuyer Credits*, GAO-12-592 (Washington, D.C.: May 29, 2012); *Service-Disabled Veteran-Owned Small Business Program: Governmentwide Fraud Prevention Control Weaknesses Leave Program Vulnerable to Fraud and Abuse, but VA Has Made Progress in Improving Its Verification Process*, GAO-12-443T (Washington, D.C.: Feb. 7, 2012); and *Energy Star Program: Covert Testing Shows the Energy Star Program Certification Process Is Vulnerable to Fraud and Abuse*, GAO-10-470 (Washington, D.C.: Mar. 5, 2010).

[49]The fraud-prevention framework was developed on the basis of findings from GAO audits of Hurricanes Katrina and Rita relief efforts and the internal control standards from the Standards for Internal Controls in the Federal Government in our prior work. See GAO-07-418T and GAO/AIMD-00-21.3.1.

holders to identify tax debt accrued after the initial clearance has been approved without having to wait until the reinvestigation.[50] Additionally, we found that some individuals misrepresented the nature of their tax debt to investigators and adjudicators. Reliance on self-reporting and the relatively time-consuming and resource-intensive investigative interviewing process presents vulnerabilities that may be mitigated by additional mechanisms to expedite the security-clearance process. A mechanism such as TOP may provide an opportunity for federal agencies to improve their identification of federal debts, including tax debts, owed by security-clearance applicants.[51] Enhancing federal agencies' access to tax-debt information for the purpose of both investigating and adjudicating security-clearance applicants, as well as ongoing monitoring of current clearance holders' tax-debt status, would better position agencies to make fully informed decisions about eligibility. This could include further exploration, through the existing working group, of routinely accessing TOP, or otherwise developing a legislative proposal, in consultation with Congress, to authorize access to tax-debt information.

Conclusions

Complete and accurate information on the tax-debt status of those applying for federal security clearances is important in helping limit potential vulnerabilities associated with granting clearances to those who might represent a security risk. Additional mechanisms to help investigative agencies access this information could help federal agencies apply the adjudicative guidelines, which call for weighing an individual's federal tax debt as it relates to an individual's financial and personal conduct when making security-clearance determinations. OPM and ODNI are currently overseeing several efforts to improve the investigative and adjudication process, including the development of a working group to explore options for establishing an automated process for reviewing federal tax compliance. As part of this effort, exploring the feasibility of investigative agencies routinely obtaining tax-debt information from the Department of the Treasury, for the purposes of investigating and adjudicating clearance applicants, as well as to conduct ongoing

---

[50]OPM officials stated that agencies will conduct continuous monitoring under Executive Order 13467 once it is fully implemented.

[51]Because TOP also contains other debt information, including delinquent child-support payments and state income-tax debts, it could also be used in determining whether the applicant accurately disclosed these other types of debts on the SF-86.

monitoring of current clearance holders' tax-debt status, could help determine how, if at all, mechanisms such as TOP could be leveraged to gain access to this information and enhance OPM's ability to conduct investigations and federal agencies' ability to assess clearance eligibility. If these methods are found to be impractical, developing a legislative proposal, in consultation with Congress, to authorize access to tax-debt information could address existing legal barriers to such information.

Recommendation for Executive Action

We recommend that, as part of its working group, the Director of National Intelligence, as the Security Executive Agent, in consultation with OPM and the Department of the Treasury, evaluate the feasibility of federal agencies routinely obtaining federal debt information from the Department of the Treasury's TOP system, or a similar automated mechanism that includes federal taxes, for the purposes of investigating and adjudicating clearance applicants, as well as for ongoing monitoring of current clearance holders' tax-debt status. If this is found to be impractical, ODNI should consider whether an exception to section 6103 is advisable and, if so, develop a legislative proposal, in consultation with Congress, to authorize access to tax-debt information.

Agency Comments and Our Evaluation

We provided a draft copy of this report to DHS, DOE, the IRS, ODNI, OPM, State, and the Department of the Treasury's Fiscal Service for their review. Letters from DHS, ODNI, and OPM are reprinted in appendixes IV, V, and VI. Both ODNI and OPM concurred with our recommendation. In its response, ODNI stated that it will recommend that the working group consider routine access of TOP for purposes of investigating, adjudicating, and monitoring security-clearance holders and applicants. This action will likely address the recommendation we proposed. If the working group determines this action is not feasible, ODNI may want to consider drafting a legislative proposal to authorize access to tax-debt information. In addition, DHS, the IRS, and OPM provided technical comments on our draft, which we incorporated as appropriate. In e-mails received on August 12, 2013, August 9, 2013, and August 8, 2013, officials from DOE, State, and the Department of the Treasury's Fiscal Service, respectively, said that they did not have any comments on the draft report.

As agreed with your offices, unless you publicly announce the contents of this report earlier, we plan no further distribution until 30 days from the report date. At that time, we will send copies to the appropriate congressional committees, the Secretary of Homeland Security, the Secretary of Energy, the Director of National Intelligence, the Director of OPM, the Secretary of State, and the Secretary of the Treasury. In addition, the report will be available at no charge on the GAO website at http://www.gao.gov.

If you or your staff have any questions about this report, please contact me at (202) 512-6722 or LordS@gao.gov. Contact points for our Offices of Congressional Relations and Public Affairs may be found on the last page of this report.

Stephen M. Lord
Director
Forensic Audits and Investigative Service

Appendix I: Federal Investigative Standards

The Office of Personnel Management (OPM), federal, or contract investigators conduct security-clearance investigations by using government-wide standards. OPM conducts background investigations for the majority of federal employees to determine their suitability for federal employment. OPM also conducts background investigations as part of the security-clearance process. For all these investigations, information that applicants provide on electronic applications is checked against numerous databases. Many investigation types contain credit and criminal-history checks, while top-secret investigations also contain citizenship, public-record, and spouse checks, as well as reference interviews and an in-person, Enhanced Subject Interview to gain insight into an applicant's character. Although it is not standard, the Enhanced Subject Interview can also be triggered for lower-level investigations if an investigation contains issues that need to be resolved in accordance with the Federal Investigative Standards. Table 1 highlights the investigative components generally associated with the suitability, and with the secret and top-secret clearance levels.

Table 1: Information Gathered in Conducting a Typical Investigation to Determine Suitability and Eligibility for a Security Clearance

Type of information gathered by component	Type of background investigation		
	Suitability	Secret	Top secret
1. Personnel security questionnaire: The reported answers on an electronic SF-85P or SF-86 form	X	X	X
2. Fingerprints: Fingerprints submitted electronically or manually	X	X	X
3. National agency check: Data from Federal Bureau of Investigation, military records, and other agencies as required	X	X	X
4. Credit check: Data from credit bureaus where the subject lived/worked/attended school for at least 6 months	X	X	X
5. Local agency checks: Data from law-enforcement agencies where the subject lived/worked/attended school during the past 10 years or—in the case of reinvestigations—since the last security-clearance investigation	V	X	X
6. Date and place of birth: Corroboration of information supplied on the personnel security questionnaire			X
7. Citizenship: For individuals born outside of the United States, verification of U.S. citizenship directly from the appropriate registration authority			X
8. Education: Verification of most-recent or significant claimed attendance, degree, or diploma	V	V	X
9. Employment: Review of employment records and interviews with workplace references, such as supervisors and coworkers	V	V	X
10. References: Data from interviews with subject-identified and investigator-developed leads	V	V	X

GAO-13-733 Security Clearances and Federal Tax Debt

Type of information gathered by component	Type of background investigation		
	Suitability	Secret	Top secret
11. National agency check for spouse or cohabitant: National agency check without fingerprint			X
12. Former spouse: Data from interview(s) conducted with spouse(s) divorced within the last 10 years or since the last investigation or reinvestigation			X
13. Neighborhoods: Interviews with neighbors and verification of residence through records check	V	V	X
14. Public records: Verification of issues, such as bankruptcy, divorce, and criminal and civil court cases			X
15. Enhanced Subject Interview: Collection of relevant data, resolution of significant issues or inconsistencies	a	a	X

Source: Department of Defense and OPM.

Legend

V = Components with this notation are checked through a mail voucher sent by OPM's Federal Investigative Services.

Notes: The content and amount of information collected as part of a personnel security-clearance investigation is dependent on a variety of case-specific factors, including the history of the applicant; however, items 1-15 are typically collected for the types of investigations indicated.

[a]The Enhanced Subject Interview was developed by the Joint Reform Team and implemented by OPM in 2011 and serves as an in-depth discussion between the interviewer and the subject to ensure a full understanding of the applicant's information, potential issues, and mitigating factors. It is included in a Moderate Risk Background Investigation, one type of suitability investigation, and can be triggered by the presence of issues in a secret-level investigation.

Appendix II: Revised Adjudicative Guidelines for Determining Eligibility for Access to Classified Information

In making determinations of eligibility for security clearances, the national-security adjudicative guidelines require adjudicators to consider (1) guidelines covering 13 specific areas of concern; (2) adverse conditions or conduct that could raise a security concern and factors that may mitigate (alleviate) the condition for each guideline; and (3) general factors related to the whole person.[1]

First, the guidelines state that eligibility determinations require an overall common-sense judgment based upon careful consideration of the following 13 guidelines in the context of the whole person:

- allegiance to the United States;
- foreign influence, such as having a family member who is a citizen of a foreign country;
- foreign preference, such as performing military service for a foreign country;
- sexual behavior;
- personal conduct, such as deliberately concealing or falsifying relevant facts when completing a security questionnaire;
- financial considerations;
- alcohol consumption;
- drug involvement;
- emotional, mental, and personality disorders;
- criminal conduct;
- security violations;
- outside activities, such as providing service to or being employed by a foreign country; and
- misuse of information-technology systems.

Second, for each of these 13 areas of concern, the guidelines specify (1) numerous significant adverse conditions or conduct that could raise a security concern that may disqualify an individual from obtaining a security clearance; and (2) mitigating factors that could allay those security concerns, even when serious, and permit granting a clearance. For example, the financial consideration guideline states that individuals

---

[1]These guidelines were established for all U.S. government civilian and military personnel, consultants, contractors, employees of contractors, licensees, certificate holders, grantees, and their employees and other individuals who require access to classified information. They apply to persons being considered for initial or continued eligibility for access to classified information, to include sensitive compartmented information and special access programs, and are to be used by government departments and agencies in all final clearance determinations.

could be denied security clearances on the basis of having a history of not meeting financial obligations. However, this security concern could be mitigated if one or more of the following factors were present: the behavior was not recent, resulted from factors largely beyond the person's control (such as loss of employment), or was addressed through counseling.

Third, the adjudicator should evaluate the relevance of an individual's overall conduct by considering the following general factors:

- the nature, extent, and seriousness of the conduct;
- the circumstances surrounding the conduct, to include knowledgeable participation;
- the frequency and recency of the conduct;
- the individual's age and maturity at the time of the conduct;
- the voluntariness of participation;
- the presence or absence of rehabilitation and other pertinent behavioral changes;
- the motivation for the conduct;
- the potential for pressure, coercion, exploitation, or duress; and
- the likelihood of continuation or recurrence.

When the personnel-security investigation uncovers no adverse security conditions, the adjudicator's task is fairly straightforward because there is no security condition to consider.

Appendix III: Scope and Methodology

Our objectives were to determine: (1) how many individuals with unpaid federal taxes, if any, are in the Office of Personnel Management (OPM) security-clearance database and what is the magnitude of any unpaid federal tax debt? and (2) to what extent do federal agencies have mechanisms to detect unpaid tax debt during the security-clearance approval process?

To determine the magnitude of unpaid federal taxes owed by individuals approved for a security clearance, we obtained and analyzed OPM data of individuals eligible for a secret or top-secret security clearance due to a favorable adjudication, either during an initial investigation or a reinvestigation, from April 1, 2006, to December 31, 2011. Our review did not include the review of confidential clearance holders or public-trust positions. Department of Energy (DOE) and U.S. Nuclear Regulatory Commission (NRC) "Q" and "L" clearances are equivalent to the top-secret and secret clearances. Thus, for the purposes of our report, we considered "Q" and "L" clearances issued by DOE and NRC to be treated as top-secret and secret clearances, respectively. We identified the OPM Central Verification System (CVS) database as the appropriate data for our analysis after meeting with OPM officials and discussing the types of data available. We used this time frame because prior to April 1, 2006, the provision of the date a clearance was granted was not required and was therefore not consistently available for analysis. OPM provided us with an extract of the OPM database that included information only on executive-branch, non–Department of Defense (DOD), and non-intelligence-community employees and contractors who were eligible for a clearance during our time frame. The OPM CVS database does not maintain information on the denial of security clearances on the basis of an individual's nonpayment of federal taxes. Thus, we were not able to determine the number of individuals who were denied security clearances for this reason. To determine the extent to which individuals eligible for a security clearance had unpaid federal taxes, we used the taxpayer identification number (TIN) as a unique identifier and electronically matched the Internal Revenue Service's (IRS) tax-debt data to the OPM data of individuals eligible for a security clearance. Specifically, we used the IRS Unpaid Assessment file as of June 30, 2012, to match against the OPM CVS data. The IRS Unpaid Assessment file used for our analysis contains all tax modules that are unpaid as of June 30, 2012. The June 30, 2012, file was used because it contained the most-recent unpaid assessment information at the time we conducted our analysis. To avoid overestimating the amount owed and to capture only significant unpaid federal taxes, we excluded from our analysis tax debts meeting specific criteria to establish a minimum threshold in the amount of tax debt to be considered when determining whether a tax debt is significant.

The criteria we used to exclude tax debts are as follows: (1) unpaid federal taxes the IRS classified as compliance assessments or memo accounts for financial reporting, and (2) recipients with total unpaid federal taxes of $100 or less. Specifically, compliance assessments or memo accounts were excluded because these taxes have neither been agreed to by the taxpayers nor affirmed by the court, or these taxes could be invalid or duplicative of other taxes already reported. We excluded tax debts of $100 or less because the IRS considers it a de minimis amount. Additionally, for the purposes of our engagement, we included individuals from the Business Master File (BMF) and Non-Master File (NMF), who were an exact Social Security number (SSN)/TIN match, as well as an exact name match with the OPM CVS data. We only included exact matches so we would be able to match and use the information from the OPM CVS database. Additionally, the Spouse Individual Master File (IMF) was not used in the magnitude analysis. This is because we were unable to determine which agency each spouse was affiliated with on the basis of the information available in both the IRS and OPM data. Additionally, the debt of a spouse may not have any effect on the security-clearance adjudication determination. As a result, the results reported may be understated.

Using these criteria, we identified about 8,400 of these individuals who had unpaid federal tax debt as of June 30, 2012. Our final estimate of tax debt does include some debt that is covered under an active IRS installment plan or beyond normal statutory time limits for debt collection. Our analysis determined the magnitude of known unpaid federal taxes owed by individuals in the OPM database and cannot be generalized to individuals that were granted eligibility for security clearances by DOD, the legislative branch, or the intelligence community.

To determine whether existing investigative and adjudication mechanisms detect unpaid tax debt during the security-clearance process and possible additional improvements to federal tax-debt detection mechanisms, we interviewed knowledgeable officials from the Office of the Director of National Intelligence (ODNI), which serves as Security Executive Agent for the federal government and has authority and responsibility over security-clearance protocols, and from OPM, which conducts security-clearance investigations for most federal agencies. In addition, we conducted interviews with officials from the Department of Homeland and Security (DHS), Department of Energy (DOE), and Department of State

(State). DHS, DOE, and State were selected because these agencies had the highest number of security clearances adjudicated from April 1, 2006, to December 31, 2011, collectively representing over 50 percent of clearances granted in OPM's CVS database, and also represented over 50 percent of the tax debt owed. In addition, we also reviewed and analyzed applicable laws, regulations, and ODNI guidance, as well as applicable policies and procedures for OPM, DHS, DOE, and State regarding the investigation and adjudication of security clearances. Finally, we conducted interviews with the Department of the Treasury's Bureau of the Fiscal Service (Fiscal Service) and the IRS to obtain their views on any initiatives and barriers in sharing tax-debt information. We compared verification mechanisms with the fraud control framework we developed in our past work and other fraud control best practices. We also used Federal Investigative Standards (see app. I) and the Adjudicative Guidelines for Determining Eligibility for Access to Classified Information (see app. II) to evaluate the current mechanisms used to identify and evaluate unpaid federal tax debt as part of the security-clearance process.

To develop case-study examples, we identified a nonprobability sample of 13 individuals for detailed reviews from the above analyses of security-clearance holders from DHS, DOE, and State who had federal tax debt. We stratified our matches using the following characteristics: (1) adjudicating agency; (2) amounts of unpaid federal taxes in the IRS Unpaid Assessment database as of June 30, 2012; (3) type of security clearance granted or approved, clearance date, and dollar amount of unpaid tax debt; and (4) whether tax debt was recorded prior to or after the security-clearance grant date. We selected 12 cases from these four strata. Additionally, we randomly selected one case with indications that IRS was assessing a trust-fund recovery penalty. Once the nonprobability sample was selected, we requested all investigative and adjudicative case-file notes from the adjudicating agency; IRS notes, detailed account transcripts, and other records from the IRS; and security-clearance files from DHS, DOE, and State for these 13 individuals. For 2 of the 13 individuals that had accrued debt only after favorable adjudication, we reviewed the adjudicative files to determine whether the agency was aware of the federal tax debt through its reinvestigation. The clearance files and IRS paperwork were systematically reviewed using a structured data-collection instrument, looking at whether the tax debt was revealed in the investigative or adjudicative processes, and, if so, how it was handled in the adjudication. Each case file was independently reviewed by two analysts. After completion of each case review, the files were compared to identify discrepancies. Potential discrepancies between case-file reviews were resolved by a third-party reviewer. These cases were selected to illustrate individuals with unpaid federal tax debt that had security clearances but the results cannot be generalized beyond the cases presented.

Data-Reliability Assessment

To assess the reliability of record-level IRS unpaid assessments data, we used the work we perform during our annual audit of the IRS's financial statements and interviewed knowledgeable IRS officials about any data-reliability issues. While our financial-statement audits have identified some data-reliability problems associated with tracing the IRS's tax records to source records and including errors and delays in recording taxpayer information and payments, we determined that the data were sufficiently reliable to address this report's objectives.

To assess the reliability of record-level OPM security-clearance data, we reviewed documentation from OPM, interviewed OPM officials who administer these information systems, and performed electronic testing of required elements. We determined that the data were sufficiently reliable to identify the individuals eligible for clearances with unpaid federal tax debt and select cases to illustrate potential vulnerabilities.

We conducted this performance audit from November 2011 to September 2013 in accordance with generally accepted government auditing standards. Those standards require that we plan and perform the audit to obtain sufficient, appropriate evidence to provide a reasonable basis for our audit findings and conclusions based on our audit objectives. We believe that the evidence obtained provides a reasonable basis for our findings and conclusions based on our audit objectives.

Appendix IV: Comments from the Department of Homeland Security

U.S. Department of Homeland Security
Washington, DC 20528

August 2, 2013

Stephen M. Lord
Director, Forensic Audits and Investigative Service
U.S. Government Accountability Office
441 G Street NW
Washington, DC 20548

Re: Draft Report GAO-13-733, "SECURITY CLEARANCES: Additional Mechanisms May Aid Federal Tax-Debt Detection"

Dear Mr. Lord:

Thank you for the opportunity to review and comment on this draft report. The U.S. Department of Homeland Security (DHS) appreciates the U.S. Government Accountability Office's (GAO's) work in planning and conducting its review and issuing this report.

DHS is pleased to note GAO's acknowledgement that agencies face challenges in detecting all unpaid federal tax debt owed by applicants in the security clearance process. Although the investigative process involves mechanisms for detecting unpaid financial obligations, including some federal tax debt, it can be difficult to identify each and every instance of unpaid debt. Reliance on self-reporting and legal restrictions on data sharing with the Internal Revenue Service complicates potential efforts to improve debt detection. Furthermore, it is not currently a condition of employment that all federal employees, regardless of whether or not they hold a clearance, be current on federal tax debt.

The Office of the Director of National Intelligence (ODNI) has convened an interagency working group to identify and address areas for improvement in the investigative process, including financial considerations. DHS has been an active participant in this process and will continue to work with ODNI and others, as appropriate, on any potential changes.

Again, thank you for the opportunity to comment on this draft report. Technical comments were previously provided under separate cover. Please feel free to contact me if you have any questions. We look forward to working with you in the future.

Sincerely,

Jim H. Crumpacker
Director
Departmental GAO-OIG Liaison Office

Appendix V: Comments from the Office of the Director of National Intelligence

OFFICE OF THE DIRECTOR OF NATIONAL INTELLIGENCE
WASHINGTON, DC 20511

Mr. Stephen M. Lord
Director
Forensic Audit and Investigative Service
Government Accountability Office
441 G Street NW
Washington, D.C. 20548

AUG 2 8 2013

Dear Mr. Lord:

The Office of the Director of National Intelligence (ODNI) appreciates the opportunity to respond to the Government Accountability Office's (GAO) draft report, *Security Clearances: Additional Mechanisms May Aid Federal Tax-Debt Detection* (GAO-13-733). GAO recommended that the Director of National Intelligence, as the Security Executive Agent, in consultation with Office of Personnel Management (OPM) and the Department of the Treasury, evaluate the feasibility of federal agencies routinely obtaining federal tax debt information. As GAO suggests, this data may be obtained from the Department of the Treasury's Offset Program (TOP) system or a similar automated mechanism that includes federal taxes for the purposes of investigating and adjudicating clearance applicants, as well as for ongoing monitoring of current clearance holders' tax-debt status. The ODNI concurs with GAO's formal recommendation for executive action.

The ODNI and OPM currently co-chair the inter-agency Federal Investigative Standards (FIS) Implementation Working Group (FISIWG) tasked to develop a phased implementation plan for the revised FIS signed in December 2012. The revised FIS require federal tax compliance checks for certain initial tiered investigations and reinvestigations. The FISIWG has engaged in ongoing discussions with Treasury and Internal Revenue Service representatives to identify potential government data sources to access federal tax compliance records while preserving the individual's privacy and civil liberties. The draft GAO report has identified TOP as another possible government data source for federal tax-debt. ODNI will recommend that the FISIWG consider routine access of TOP for the purposes of investigating and adjudicating clearance applicants, as well as for ongoing monitoring of current clearance holders' tax-debt status.

Sincerely,

Deborah G. Barger
Director of Legislative Affairs

Appendix VI: Comments from the Office of Personnel Management

UNITED STATES OFFICE OF PERSONNEL MANAGEMENT
Washington, DC 20415

The Director

JUN 2 0 2013

Stephen M. Lord
Director, Forensic Audits and Investigative Service
United States Government Accountability Office
441 G Street NW
Washington, DC 20548

Dear Mr. Lord:

Thank you for providing the U.S. Office of Personnel Management (OPM) the opportunity to respond to the Government Accountability Office (GAO) draft report "Security Clearances: Additional Mechanisms May Aid Federal Tax-Debt Detection (GAO-13-733)."

Recommendations for Executive Action

We recommend that, as part of its working group, the Director of National Intelligence, as the Security Executive Agent, in consultation with OPM and the Department of the Treasury, evaluate the feasibility of Federal agencies routinely obtaining Federal debt information from the Department of the Treasury's TOP system, or a similar automated mechanism that includes Federal taxes, for the purposes of investigating and adjudicating clearance applicants, as well as for ongoing monitoring of current clearance holders' tax-debt status. If this is found to be impractical, ODNI should consider whether an exception to section 6103 is advisable and, if so, develop a legislative proposal, in consultation with Congress, to authorize access to tax-debt information.

OPM Response

OPM concurs with the recommendation that we assist the Director of National Intelligence, the Security Executive Agent, as part of its working group, in evaluating the feasibility of Federal agencies routinely obtaining Federal debt information from the Department of the Treasury's TOP system for the purposes expressed. We are appreciative of the opportunity to provide technical comments, which we provided separately on August 14. Attached for your consideration are additional comments from OPM's Office of General Counsel.

We appreciate the time and effort that GAO put into this review and welcome the opportunity to improve processes for investigating clearance applicants as recommended.

Please do not hesitate to contact me if you have additional questions.

Sincerely,

Elaine Kaplan
Acting Director

Attachment

Related GAO Products

Personnel Security Clearances: Further Actions Needed to Improve the Process and Realize Efficiencies. GAO-13-728T. Washington, D.C.: June 20, 2013.

Medicaid: Providers in Three States with Unpaid Federal Taxes Received over $6 Billion in Medicaid Reimbursements. GAO-12-857. Washington, D.C.: July 27, 2012.

Security Clearances: Agencies Need Clearly Defined Policy for Determining Civilian Position Requirements. GAO-12-800. Washington, D.C.: July 12, 2012.

Personnel Security Clearances: Continuing Leadership and Attention Can Enhance Momentum Gained from Reform Effort. GAO-12-815T. Washington, D.C.: June 21, 2012.

Recovery Act: Tax Debtors Have Received FHA Mortgage Insurance and First-Time Homebuyer Credits. GAO-12-592. Washington, D.C.: May 29, 2012.

Recovery Act: Thousands of Recovery Act Contract and Grant Recipients Owe Hundreds of Millions in Federal Taxes. GAO-11-485. Washington, D.C.: April 28, 2011.

Federal Tax Collection: Potential for Using Passport Issuance to Increase Collection of Unpaid Taxes. GAO-11-272. Washington, D.C.: March 10, 2011.

Medicare: Thousands of Medicare Providers Abuse the Federal Tax System. GAO-08-618. Washington, D.C.: June 13, 2008.

Tax Compliance: Federal Grant and Direct Assistance Recipients Who Abuse the Federal Tax System. GAO-08-31. Washington, D.C.: November 16, 2007.

Medicaid: Thousands of Medicaid Providers Abuse the Federal Tax System. GAO-08-17. Washington, D.C.: November 14, 2007.

Tax Compliance: Thousands of Organizations Exempt from Federal Income Tax Owe Nearly $1 Billion in Payroll and Other Taxes. GAO-07-1090T. Washington, D.C.: July 24, 2007.

Tax Compliance: Thousands of Organizations Exempt from Federal Income Tax Owe Nearly $1 Billion in Payroll and Other Taxes. GAO-07-563. Washington, D.C.: June 29, 2007.

Tax Compliance: Thousands of Federal Contractors Abuse the Federal Tax System. GAO-07-742T. Washington, D.C.: April 19, 2007.

Medicare: Thousands of Medicare Part B Providers Abuse the Federal Tax System. GAO-07-587T. Washington, D.C.: March 20, 2007.

GAO's Mission	The Government Accountability Office, the audit, evaluation, and investigative arm of Congress, exists to support Congress in meeting its constitutional responsibilities and to help improve the performance and accountability of the federal government for the American people. GAO examines the use of public funds; evaluates federal programs and policies; and provides analyses, recommendations, and other assistance to help Congress make informed oversight, policy, and funding decisions. GAO's commitment to good government is reflected in its core values of accountability, integrity, and reliability.
Obtaining Copies of GAO Reports and Testimony	The fastest and easiest way to obtain copies of GAO documents at no cost is through GAO's website (http://www.gao.gov). Each weekday afternoon, GAO posts on its website newly released reports, testimony, and correspondence. To have GAO e-mail you a list of newly posted products, go to http://www.gao.gov and select "E-mail Updates."
Order by Phone	The price of each GAO publication reflects GAO's actual cost of production and distribution and depends on the number of pages in the publication and whether the publication is printed in color or black and white. Pricing and ordering information is posted on GAO's website, http://www.gao.gov/ordering.htm. Place orders by calling (202) 512-6000, toll free (866) 801-7077, or TDD (202) 512-2537. Orders may be paid for using American Express, Discover Card, MasterCard, Visa, check, or money order. Call for additional information.
Connect with GAO	Connect with GAO on Facebook, Flickr, Twitter, and YouTube. Subscribe to our RSS Feeds or E-mail Updates. Listen to our Podcasts. Visit GAO on the web at www.gao.gov.
To Report Fraud, Waste, and Abuse in Federal Programs	Contact: Website: http://www.gao.gov/fraudnet/fraudnet.htm E-mail: fraudnet@gao.gov Automated answering system: (800) 424-5454 or (202) 512-7470
Congressional Relations	Katherine Siggerud, Managing Director, siggerudk@gao.gov, (202) 512-4400, U.S. Government Accountability Office, 441 G Street NW, Room 7125, Washington, DC 20548
Public Affairs	Chuck Young, Managing Director, youngc1@gao.gov, (202) 512-4800 U.S. Government Accountability Office, 441 G Street NW, Room 7149 Washington, DC 20548

Please Print on Recycled Paper.